LIFE LESSONS

LIFE LESSONS

What Parenting, Education, and Relationships Teach Us

AVERY NIGHTINGALE

Creative Quill Press

CONTENTS

CHAPTER 1

Parenting

Communication between parent and child is the most important factor for the good growth of the child. It is often said that a child's mind is like clay and that it can be molded in whichever way you want. But today's generation has another saying that it's the parents who have to shape their minds by connecting with them at the child's level. This includes talking to children about various issues, ranging from their school work, their friends, their teachers, any current incidents in the world, and the child's role in it. Any problem faced by the child in today's world needs good advice from the parents, which can only be given if the child is able to open up their mind to the parent. This activity also includes decision making for the child, which might affect the child but should still be decided by the parent. Then, considering the child's mind, take steps that do not create ill effects on the child, and if it does, the parent should explain the reality to the child.

Parenting is a term that can be described as the governance of children by parents until the child is capable of taking care of and maintaining themselves. It includes various activities that are done by the parent to ensure that the child gets on the right path to becoming a matured individual one day and taking on responsibilities that may be greater than what the parents currently have. Any activity that involves teaching a child something, right from how to feed themselves to teaching them how to earn, is said to be a part of parenting. It has been typically divided into "good nurturing of a child" and "bad nurturing of a child" depending on the activities done by the parents towards the child.

1.1. Importance of Communication

Communication is the key to any healthy relationship. A child learns how to communicate from his/her parents, primarily from observing and imitating them. If a child observes a parent using healthy communication skills with others and the child, he/she will copy the same pattern. The child begins to form his/her communication style by watching and listening to others. When a parent talks to a child, he/she believes in what they have to say (even if it is not what the child wants to hear), the child feels worthy and understood. As a result, the child develops a willingness to open up and express his/her thoughts and feelings. Effective communication and the child feeling worthy and understood are the building blocks to establishing a good relationship between the parent and child. This is important for when the child becomes a teenager and must face difficult decisions and experiences. If an adolescent has established effective communication with his/her parents, studies show they are less likely to use or abuse drugs, have sex early, or participate in delinquent activities. Overall, research has shown that a positive and open parent/child communication can influence an adolescent to make good choices and have a lower level of psychological distress. An effort towards healthy communication continues to be important throughout the child's life, even when the child becomes an adult. This is due to parents continuing to do what they have always done for their child and so the level and type of communication does not change. This is reflected in ageless adults and their aging parents. Effective communication can influence a child to care for and make good decisions for his/her elderly parent.

1.2. Setting Boundaries and Discipline

Understanding what the child's goal at the time of the offense often requires a bit of detective work, as children get better at covering up misbehavior as they get older. Parents must examine what has caused the behavior, often stemming from factors such as fatigue, hunger, boredom, anger, seeking attention, and various emotional factors, which serve to make identification of misbehavior causes slightly complex. A child's readiness to misbehave on a bad day when rules aren't any different shows that their internal motivation for misbehavior is high, and on the contrary, low incidences of misbehavior when in a particularly engaging event, an indicator that their misbehavior, not the rule, is a problem. By determining when and why the misbehavior is occurring, it is easier to understand which rules need to be enforced more than others, and which situations need to be avoided if misbehavior is more likely to occur.

Setting boundaries and discipline is important to every household, primarily because all children need to know where they stand and what is expected of them. This is no small feat when considering how best to accomplish this. Most adults find it easiest to simply punish when rules are broken, often using whatever punishment makes them angry to any degree. One must understand that consequences for negative behavior should not be used simply to penalize children, but rather to dissuade repeated offenses. "The penalty needs to be related, not to the seriousness of the action, but to the child's goal at the time". It is only truly effective when it actually stops the behavior.

1.3. Nurturing Emotional Intelligence

This is best achieved by responding warmly and consistently to the child. A child's warmth wanting to signal that they are distressed or that they have achieved something is known as a bid for emotional contact. It might range from a baby's cry to a teenager excitedly telling about an accomplishment. If the mother acknowledges the child's words or behavior with equal or greater warmth, this will lead to the development of emotional intelligence. However, if she disregards the bid or tries to brush aside the child's emotions, the child will learn that emotions are not to try to reroute someone else's mental state and emotions can have unforeseen and unintended effects. They may decide that anger is not worth displaying and begin to suppress future feelings of anger. This can be a double-edged sword. For example, anger to aggression translates to someone wanting to elicit discomfort in another person (from a situation that caused the first person discomfort), and this anger is too readily displayed by adolescents. The mom may well love the fact that her child never gets angry but will have difficulty in preventing him from turning into a walkover.

The process of nurturing emotional intelligence starts in the cradle. The first relationship that the child develops, usually is with the mother. Emotional intelligence needs to be developed in that relationship.

The concept of emotional intelligence is relatively new in psychological research, yet there are few subjects so far that are as important to parenting and the lifelong development of children. What is emotional intelligence? Emotional intelligence is the capacity to recognize, understand, and manage our own emotions and to recognize, understand, and influence the emotions of others. It's not about being soft. It's about understanding emotion's language.

1.4. Balancing Love and Independence

Every good parent knows that they love their child unconditionally. What parents find problematic is how to take that love they feel and translate it into actions that raise a child who is responsible and self-disciplined. Many parents accede to their children's wishes when they know they should not because they do not want to do anything that might hurt their child's feelings. Other parents punish their children but do so out of anger and frustration, and not out of love. This raises the question of how to best show a child that they are loved. A good balance of showing love and affection and setting boundaries and discipline is crucial. This balance often changes as the child grows and moves through different stages in development. It is easy for parents to show love to a child who is compliant and does what they want. It is much more difficult when dealing with a child who is disobedient. This is where many adults struggle and is also where many children develop misconceptions about their parents' love for them. Young children, especially under the age of 6, are very concrete in their thinking and tend to think that good behavior will bring rewards and bad behavior will bring punishment. This can be problematic if a child feels that they are being punished because their parents are mean or do not love them. This is why it is so important to discipline out of love and to talk to the child explaining that it is their behavior you are unhappy with and not them. A good relationship and open communication will make it easier for a child to understand this.

1.5. Teaching Responsibility and Accountability

The word accountability is often used synonymously with responsibility; however, it is important to differentiate the two. Accountability can be defined as answerability, with the ability to explain or justify a particular event or outcome. This is particularly relevant for this period of time when parents manipulate a child's behavior using praise, reward, incentive, or disapproval and punishment to encourage the taking on of responsibilities and development of good habits. In contrast to praise, punishment is less desirable as it is a method by which children may come to avoid taking responsibility for their actions and instead shift responsibility onto the avoidance of the punishment itself. In turn, this leads to a sense of learned helplessness, where an individual believes his actions cannot affect an outcome.

It is advisable to allow children to ever increasingly take responsibility for certain tasks, in turn providing an appropriate level of support and guidance to ensure they can complete the task to the best of their ability. The aim is to find a balance between taking over when mistakes are inevitable and allowing natural consequences (that are not harmful to the child or others) to occur from the child's action or inaction. When an error occurs, it is important not to resort to punishment but instead focus upon problem-solving, ensuring that the child understands what went wrong and what can be done better next time.

Our inability to take responsibility for our mistakes and failures has led to an attitude of blaming other people or our circumstances for our inability to perform optimally and maintain successful relationships.

This, in turn, leads to disempowerment both in ourselves and in the minds of others about what we are capable of achieving. It is during childhood that we begin to form attitudes towards responsibility, which will, by and large, determine how and in what manner we pursue our personal and professional goals.

1.6. Instilling Values and Morals

Children obtain values and morals from their surroundings. Home and school are the most influential places for kids. As education begins at home, parents are the first influential figures in a child's life. Parents must start early in teaching their children. Moral is when you do what is right. Value is when you do the right thing, and it is easy to do. The worth and level of understanding of values will increase as the child matures. Latecomers see many things happening around them which ignite conflicts of interest between what they have been taught and what other children do who haven't learned their morals. Often, they become critical of their own values and others too. This critical status, if not handled carefully, may lead the child to engage in negative values. This is the period when value education is very essential. Various strategic and trial and error methods must be executed by parents to understand the most effective way to instill values in them. Effectively promoting the exchange of thoughts and citing examples should be more beneficial. Always be a role model and practice what is preached. Daily reminders and instilling should not cease. Parents should continuously monitor the child and continuously evaluate the child, which is very important and the only way to seek out the teenager's newly formed values and ease the shifting of them up to higher level values. The child should also be informed of the consequences of practicing the values and the impact on his life. The child's understanding level will take quite a long time to fathom. Parents need not stop until they can confidently say, "My child is value educated." Another primary method is through religious and spiritual effort. The individual will understand the relative concept of sin and virtue as said in his religion and slowly develop the interest to practice good and avoid unpleasant things. Another way is by participating in community service events, which is more about putting virtue into practice. Encourage the child to think about what is right in difficult situations. The ability to make the right decision when caught up in a critical situation entirely depends on how the value system has been inculcated in the child up to this point. He should be told to see the positives and negatives of his decision and how that would affect him and others. This decision-making ability is what strongly reflects the possession of a value system. Though this path is very critical, the final success is assured. Moral is a very sensitive issue and continuous care should be taken to ensure that the child does not practice negative things. This is actually a challenging experience in every parent's life who always desires their child to be good and may take a long time starting from childhood until the youth attains maturity. But it is never a wasted effort and as they say, "Hard work always bears sweet fruits." In due course, the value system will reflect in each and every action of the child, behavior, and personality. He would win the praises of teachers and other parents, and the realization of satisfactory return of successful value education can be experienced. This is the right point to recognize that parents have completed an important task, something really incomparable for their child. The child's understanding of the imbibed value education and realizing the parents' effort will certainly be a great happy moment for the parent. They can relax with satisfaction, saying "We did our duty well."

CHAPTER 2

Education

With the current education policy stressing the importance of English and Maths, it is essential that students learning these subjects are able to learn how to think critically. Critical thinking is a vital skill for humans as we are constantly faced with decisions and problems in a day. By learning how to think critically, a person can be sure to avoid making bad decisions and find the most effective way to solve problems. Once mastered, the skill of critical thinking is something that can be applied to many aspects of life to attain a deeper understanding of a matter and to make better judgments.

As a person gets older and aims to enter into education, critical thinking is defined as active, persistent, and careful consideration of a belief or supposed form of knowledge in the light of the grounds that support it and the further conclusions to which it tends. This can be translated to mean being able to question knowledge and beliefs, the ability to learn new things, and to discover new possibilities. This is key in becoming a well-educated person who is able to contribute greatly to society.

As Life Lessons: What Parenting, Education, and Relationships Teach Us mentions, the education system. From the moment a person is born, they are given opportunities to learn every day, but the way that a person is taught is said to begin at the age of three. Through relationship experiences that a person encounters with siblings and friends, children begin to develop the ability to have an open mind and explore different ways to think, a characteristic that is crucial to critical thinking.

2.1. Lifelong Learning

Lifetime learners are further characterized by their learning motivation. A strong intrinsic motivation to obtain knowledge and achieve is what separates learning from mere schooling. Developing a strong student who is an active problem solver, information-sensitive, and highly motivated is a daunting task in today's fast food entertainment videogame society. However, the development of these learning skills is the essence of what is required for future employability and continuous knowledge and skill update.

Recognizing the need for a new learning skill set, we must cultivate youth learners who can navigate through an information-dense environment in search of knowledge. Traditional instructional methods emphasizing rote memorization and repetitious practice will not develop the information processing and problem-solving skills needed in the future job market. Lifetime learners are active learners who have strong thinking, metacognitive, and problem-solving skills. This literally means they have the ability to think about their own thinking and apply strategies to obtain knowledge and solve problems. Lifetime learners are also information-sensitive individuals who have the ability to access, evaluate, and synthesize information. Obtaining information and knowledge from a near-infinite database requires certain information processing skills.

In looking at the rapid escalation of knowledge change, a strong case can be made that "the half-life of a learned skill is becoming shorter and shorter". This simply means that the amount of knowledge an individual possesses is becoming less important than their ability to learn. Lifelong learners will be those who will remain in demand in this type of environment. This has vast implications on how we must educate children from this point forward. We are required to equip them with the skills, motivation, and love of learning necessary for continuous skill and knowledge update throughout an entire lifetime. Lifetime learning skills characterized by self-directed learning will need to become the new educational standard.

In today's high-paced knowledge-based society, the mastery of "techniques of production" has been diminished in importance, and the development of continuous learning skills has taken on a critical role. The pace of change is making the skills and knowledge for an employee obsolete at a faster rate. Additionally, global competition is redefining the knowledge and skill requirements for maintaining a high standard of living. It is clear that the average lifespan of knowledge of an educated person today is declining. Most experts agree on the vast implications this has on employability, career development, and job security.

2.2. Developing Critical Thinking Skills

The activity provided below is a method for a history course. The teacher described its overall objective as follows: to develop students' abilities to think historically, to connect from fragmentary and confusing evidence the meaningful intelligible structures of past societies, cultures, and bio-physical worlds in a way that may change their understanding in meaningful ways, and to evaluate the often more awfulness of the utilization of past learning to today's problems and potentialities. This description sets a solid and appropriate developmental objective for critical thinking which could potentially be applied to a whole course curriculum.

Faculty members trying any program to enhance critical thinking must build in stages of skill development, making sure there's internal motivation to reach training and ample opportunity to practice skills. This can be done through a lot of exercises, many of which require application and analysis rather than simple recall or comprehension.

Doing college work is not a guarantee one will learn to think in a certain way, nor is the purchase of a sizable portion of theory at the start of one's college career. Critical thinking develops only after solid practice using the skills with proper motivation. Most college students in one study did not enhance their critical thinking abilities by the end of their sophomore year. On average, students in this study mentioned that their abilities in applying knowledge, critical thinking, and analytic reasoning increased only slightly from their freshman to senior years.

Developing Critical Thinking Skills - The content of the term critical thinking and then recommends a developmental method to instruct it.

2.3. Embracing Failure and Resilience

The ability to fail and pick oneself up again is something that is ingrained in the mind of every martial artist and those who have come to understand exactly what it is that they practice. Everyone is aware of the fact that through understanding it is possible to gain a great deal of skill. Yet many fear failure to the extent that they will not endeavor to learn new things in which they know that they will not be initially successful. This creates a mindset of stagnation where people will only operate with what knowledge they have, leading to a dead-end street of skill development. Students and even instructors must always remember that a black belt is a white belt that never gave up. The only difference between the esteemed black belt and the novice white belt is a measure of time and numerous mistakes made along the way. The black belt may have forgotten the days of the countless times they fell on their rear attempting a hip throw, or became dizzy and disoriented trying to find a way out of a particular ground escape. But it is well understood that the learning process is what separates the two. By embracing failure as a necessary part of learning we are able to let go of our egos and the need to constantly be recognized as skilled and knowledgeable. This is what frees us to truly immerse ourselves in the deep waters of true understanding and self-improvement.

2.4. Fostering Creativity and Imagination

In discussing imagination, education and child development expert Jean Piaget stated, "Imagination is more important than knowledge." While it can be argued that this statement is somewhat idealistic, there is certainly a lot of truth in it and as the emphasis on project-based learning increases, allowing children to think imaginatively will be an important part of their development.

This is particularly important in education as children move to more project-based work. In a society where information is no longer scarce, those with the ability to think of new and innovative ways to use that information will be the ones to succeed. It is likely that our current education system is a hindrance to this; teachers' concerns over league tables and exam results often mean that children are not given the time or resources to think of creative solutions to problems. This is an area in which home learning could be particularly beneficial. An example could be in giving your child a complex puzzle or problem to solve and asking them to think of as many different ways to solve it as possible, highlighting that divergent thinking is an important part of creativity.

Like so many of the other traits discussed in this paper, focusing on creativity and imagination will help children in a variety of subject areas as well as in later life. Creativity is not just about art; the most creative scientists and mathematicians are able to think of new and innovative ideas. As stated in the National Advisory Committee on Creative and Cultural Education, "Intelligence and cognitive development are not the same thing." In this quote, it is implied that creative development is still an important part of intelligence. Creativity can lead to further cognitive development but it is also a way to utilize intelligence in a more free and unstructured capacity.

2.5. Promoting Collaboration and Teamwork

Fostering teamwork and collaboration isn't restricted to children. In this world of TEKS, testing, and high-stakes accountability, teachers these days have to make a concerted effort to build in lessons and activities designed to foster teamwork. There are countless team building activities that have been effective, but to name a few, two of my favorites are the classic egg drop and a trebuchet building contest. Unfortunately, school can also be a breeding ground for negative forms of competition, and teamwork and collaboration are often put aside in order to get a better individual grade. One attempt to counteract this insidious trend is the adaptation of learning to students' beloved video games. My sixth-grade team has been having enormous success holding Civilization III game days. Yes, I know it's a video game, but the amount of critical thinking and teamwork involved in this game almost makes it an educational experience. Any doubts about that from parents can be assuaged by the fact that the kids come away with better knowledge of the basics of world history. Much work still remains to bring my kids to their optimal level of teamwork, but they have made great progress to this point and are, in essence, learning that two heads are better than one.

Collaboration and teamwork can take many forms. For my children, learning to work together has spanned from simple board games and creating LEGO masterpieces to putting on full costumes and acting out elaborate role-plays. Often times, it begins with a vision one of them has and they quickly realize that in order for their grand idea to come to fruition they must pool their creative resources. The beauty of children is their simple joy in doing things with one another. Almost any-thing can be a tool for learning collaboration. One particularly effective one for teaching teamwork was the construction and completion of a marble roller-coaster track. This ageless activity has been adapted to so many projects there should be a gubernatorial proclamation declaring it the state project of Texas. Any Texan who reads this and tries the marble roller coaster project, please let me know the results. Another recent foray into teamwork has been learning chess. They are just beginning to grasp the complexities of this game as well as the fact that their father still hasn't let them win. When they began to succeed in outmaneu-vering me, this opened up a whole new dimension of the game with various role reversals and plays on multiple games running concurrently in order to remember the positions of the pieces.

2.5. Promoting Collaboration and Teamwork

2.6. Cultivating a Growth Mindset

"Ash Gavzey" is a prime example of a sports teacher with a growth mindset, and has a truly aspirational tale. Knowing nothing about the sport, he took on a rowing coaching role at a struggling state school, with the intentions of creating a more inclusive and accessible college sports program. He accepted that it was going to be a hard and long process, but was prepared to fight for future success. Later taking up a role at King's College, he persistently tried new ideas and coaching techniques in order to improve his students, often with little immediate success. After a personal re-enactment of Steve Redgrave's 5th Olympic gold medal retirement-unretirement, he accomplished an extraordinary feat by taking a state school crew to the semi-finals at the Schools Head, an event normally dominated by private schools. This success was achieved through unwavering determination, hard work, and the belief that failure was never a setback, but merely a stepping-stone to success. He promoted the same attitude to his rowers, one which Dweck would be proud of.

Dweck describes how people with a fixed mindset say things like "this is too hard" or "I would be a natural at that." Such people are overly concerned with looking smart - this is the be-all and end-all for them. Conversely, those with a growth mindset will view the world as a place full of opportunity. They will relish the chance to embark on something new and challenging, seeing any initial failures as a stepping stone to future success. In this way, teachers too can be categorized under these mindsets. Those with a fixed mindset will feel that their true potential has already been reached, and so will be less inclined to put extra effort into further developing their teaching ability. On the other hand, a teacher with a growth mindset will constantly be searching for ways to improve their students' learning, through the improvement of their own teaching skills. The ultimate goal is to persuade teachers to install a growth mindset into their students, by being a living example of this themselves.

So you see, it's not just children who should learn from their mistakes - teachers should do the same. If a child fails to understand something, it's a teacher's responsibility to understand it from the child's point of view, in order to teach it in a different way next time. Teachers should be willing to take the risk of experimenting with new teaching styles and methods in order to ensure better learning for their students. The old adage for the student "I've tried my best and it's no good" should be replaced with "I've not tried my best and I need to do something about it".

2.7. Adapting to Change and Continuous Improvement

Change is an inevitable and inescapable part of life. However, some changes occur gradually or rapidly, and often these changes force an individual to adapt and adjust in new learning and personal environments. The ability to adapt and develop strategies for continuous improvement is an essential skill to possess in today's modern world. To be effective lifelong learners, students must possess self-regulation skills and effective problem-solving strategies to monitor and manage their own learning experiences. This can involve setting and planning realistic personal goals, being flexible in strategies to achieve those goals, utilizing time management and task structuring skills, being able to self-evaluate and adapt given new information and undertaking alternative strategies, and recognizing and overcoming personal beliefs and psychological barriers that may impede change and development. Students who engage in these self-regulatory behaviors for the purpose of enhancing their academic competencies exhibit more adaptive patterns of cognition and behavior and a deeper understanding of effective learning strategies. This has a direct link with higher academic achievement, greater motivation and increased confidence in one's ability to learn and perform. An Australian study identified that students with a strong mastery orientation are more likely to seek out challenges in the face of failure and adapt more constructive coping strategies such as attributing failure to controllable factors. This contrasts with learned helplessness, where a student has a maladaptive pattern of behavior characterized by a fear of failure and a general avoidance of challenging tasks. Such students are more likely to have a performance orientation and exhibit self-handicapping behaviors in the learning environment. This is clearly undesirable for students in working to achieve their personal best and attain higher education.

CHAPTER 3

Relationships

Relationships are what sustain humanity and are the basis for all communities. They can be powerfully fulfilling or painstakingly destructive, depending on the skills one has developed. Relationships are built on the foundation of trust. In parent/child relationships, trust is integral in the early years of the child's development. Parents must protect their children from harm, both physical and emotional, and be reliable in their care. Should this occur, a secure child-parent attachment is likely to form. Children will want to seek comfort and share experiences with their parents, and the child will view the parents as a "safe haven". The secure attachment will provide the child with a healthy role model for future relationships. The child will have learned about trust and reciprocity in emotions, thus allowing effective communication in their future relationships. Trust can also be attained in adult relationships, after hardships or when first established, through the ability to be vulnerable. One must have confidence in the empathy and compassion from their partner in order to confide, and this often strengthens the bond between two people.

3.1. Building Trust and Communication

It is important to be able to approach these types of conversations with an open mind and a neutral stance. This will prepare for an experience of shared emotional understanding where both parties will feel comfortable expressing their thoughts and emotions on said issue. It is very important during these conversations to practice empathy and try to see the situation from the other's point of view. This will avoid any misunderstandings and help to clarify any points of miscommunication.

Trust can be easily broken, so it is always important to gauge the level of trust from the other person and to not act in any way that may compromise the level of trust that has been reached. Communication is the key to every relationship, and open, honest communication is the way to finding understanding and establishing mutual rapport. The ability to communicate and openly discuss any difficult or uncomfortable topic is a skill that takes time to develop. People are often too quick to become defensive or place blame in a situation that makes them feel uncomfortable. By doing this, they inhibit resolution of the issue and only succeed in creating emotional hurt and often damaging the relationship.

In society today, for many, trust doesn't come easily due to past experiences which may be mirrored onto the current relationship. Because of this, it is essential to be patient and persistent, never consenting that trust cannot be gained. Open and honest communication is a way to amend any past issues that inhibit the development of trust. If communication is open and forthcoming, clarity is given to the intention of every action and information can be provided to clear up any misunderstandings that may be causing apprehension in the relationship.

Trust is often labeled as the most fundamental part of a relationship, as it sets the groundwork for future interactions. Trust often comes from within. The individual must feel secure with oneself before expecting trust from others. The other most effective way of gaining trust is to show that you are trustworthy through the way in which you conduct yourself. Through what you say and the way you conduct yourself, a feeling of security from the other party relies on this. This feeling of security is what trust evolves from.

3.2. Respecting Differences and Empathy

Respecting differences and empathy are important in order for relationships to grow. At a young age, I was faced with a constant problem of needing to fit in with my peers. Whether it was the type of kiddy lunch I brought to school or the way I presented myself, I always felt the need to change in order to please others, striving to be like everyone else and mold myself to society's standards. How were they different from me? Why did I need to be exactly like them in order to get along? These were the questions that constantly ran through my mind. As I grew, I came to realize that people are innately different, and the differences between us are what add variety to our lives. Instead of blending and changing to be like others, it is essential to embrace individuality and to show respect for others' differences. In order to teach children to respect diversity, parents or educators must lead by example. It is important to eliminate any personal prejudices they may have and to promote an environment that is open-minded and tolerant. Empathy enables one to understand the emotions and perspectives of others and is an important tool for working towards compromise and understanding. During a conflict, people often are biased towards their own feelings and fail to see the other person's side. Encouraging a child to take a moment to put themselves in the other person's shoes will help them to understand the opposing perspective and work towards a solution. An example of an exercise in empathy is an activity that a teacher once had my class complete. She had two of my classmates sit back to back, one person being the speaker and the other the listener. The speaker was to tell a story of a personal experience while the listener drew a picture of the story. Afterwards, the listener would share their picture and the two would compare to see how each interpreted the story. This activity helps children to learn that people can have differing views of the same situation and that it is important to understand the perspective of others.

3.3. Managing Conflict and Compromise

This is an area where many people struggle, often defaulting back to anger and frustration. It is important as parents and educators to display healthy conflict resolution as children are extremely perceptive and will often adopt poor conflict resolution styles if not shown a healthy alternative. Compromise is also an essential skill in maintaining positive relationships and should be practiced often. Whether it be a compromise in discipline or finding a middle ground on family decisions, showing children that a compromise can be satisfying for both parties is an invaluable lesson. An example may be a teenager wanting to extend their curfew, the parents may be uncomfortable with this initially and say no. A healthy compromise would be to extend the curfew but have an extra job for the teenager to do to make up for the later time. This teaches the teenager valuable work ethic and responsibility skills, important life skills that may not have been taught otherwise.

3.4. Cultivating Healthy Boundaries

Setting boundaries always begins with awareness. We need to be aware of what feels comfortable and what does not feel comfortable for us, and we need to take time to listen to and trust our feelings on this. Often it means taking some quiet time for ourselves while we reflect on our true feelings and desires about our relationships and the decisions we have to make.

The first step in cultivating a boundary is assessing what makes you feel uncomfortable or where your resentment lies. How others relate to us are often our biggest clues to knowing what our boundaries are. If we've ever felt used, it's because we didn't set a boundary. We can tell because whenever we think of that situation, we'll feel a twinge in our gut; it's a physical effect. Anger, a signal that our boundaries have been crossed, or anxiety, depression, and feelings of helplessness, all show us where we need to set limits. Boundaries are usually set to preserve or improve our own well-being, so it is important to know that you have a right and it is your responsibility to set them.

Lastly, when we have firm and healthy boundaries, we are free to express love and affection because we are not acting out of fear or guilt, and we are not enabling, rescuing, or taking on someone else's responsibilities.

Without clear boundaries, miscommunications will result. It will be unclear where you end and the other person begins. This can result in a great deal of stress, anxiety, and even conflict. When others do not respect our boundaries, or we theirs, and we end up doing things we do not really want to do, this can lead to feelings of anger, guilt, and resentment. Clarity about boundaries can help us to be assertive, act in integrity with our true self, and make balanced decisions. A lack of boundaries is like leaving the door to our home unlocked; it can be an invitation for intruders to come in and it doesn't stop the ones we want out from coming in.

The ability to set healthy personal boundaries is an important aspect of creating any healthy relationship. In general, "boundary" is a limit or space between you and the other person; a clear place where you begin and the other person ends.

3.5. Practicing Active Listening

The problem with many of us is that we don't listen to understand; we listen to reply. When we listen to reply, we use the time when another person is explaining their problem to think about a solution to the problem or something else entirely. At some stage, we may be so eager to offer help that we offer it before the other person has finished explaining the problem. Then we find the other person feels that we have not understood the problem fully and feel that we are pushing our own solution to their issue without full understanding. All these conflicts can be avoided if we put the time into fully listening and understanding the problem as the speaker presents it.

Active listening is an essential tool for understanding people and their concerns. It's more than simply hearing the words that are being said; it involves paying attention to the whole person - including what isn't said and what isn't easy to say. Active listening can improve personal relationships by reducing conflicts, strengthening cooperation, and fostering understanding. It can also help solve problems and resolve conflicts in a way that is respectful to everyone involved.

3.6. Nurturing Love and Affection

In communicating with our children, it is important to offer more love than correction. A good goal is to offer 5-6 times as much positive reinforcement and encouragement as we do pointing out their mistakes and what they should do instead. This can be hard to do when we are using discipline to change behaviors that are problematic. However, constant correction is hard on a child's spirit and it can lead to discouragement and resentment. When the child is not misbehaving, let him know what a wonderful pleasure it is for you to be with him and how much you appreciate his cooperation. A healthy self-concept is the greatest gift we can give our children, and encouragement is the most effective way to nurture self-confidence. Sincere praise and positive encouragement foster the sense of being loved. A loved child is more likely to act in ways that are lovable.

By searching to understand the need and empathizing with the child, we are better able to discipline with love and effect lasting change in behavior. When children see that we are making an effort to figure out their feelings, it communicates that we really do care about how they feel. This, in turn, makes them feel special and loved. The more special a child feels in your presence and the more he believes that you are acting in his best interests, the more willingly he will cooperate.

To maintain healthy relationships with our children and other important people in our lives, we need to intentionally nurture them with love and affection. This can be difficult to do with our children when we are extremely angry with their behavior. This is when the behavior is least lovable, but when the child probably has the greatest need for feeling loved. It is important in these moments to remind ourselves that it is our child's behavior that we are angry with, not the child. "It is more productive to view misbehavior simply as your child's unsuccessful attempt to meet a need."

3.7. Sustaining Long-lasting Connections

Sometimes change separates people, whether it is physical relocation or a shift in values or interests, thereby rendering the original context of the relationship outdated. In an effort to sustain the connection, it may be necessary to redefine the relationship with a new context. If distance is the issue, continued long-distance communication is essential. Frequent or scheduled communication will show the other person is still of importance. If feasible, visits to or from the person in question are a great way to maintain physical presence. If successful, it may be possible to create new shared experiences, effectively returning to the aforementioned strategy. Circumstances may take a change for the worst if common or shared interests are lost. This may be prevented by taking up new mutual hobbies and interests or introducing the other party to some of your own. Remember that any change in the nature of the relationship is an opportunity to strengthen the existing bond by means of a new understanding or common goal.

Often the easiest way to maintain a connection is simply through the presence of face-to-face interaction. Maintaining regular contact with friends or relatives prevents feelings of detachment and insulation. Picking up the phone for a random call shows your willingness to stay in touch and solidifies the notion that you are a dependable friend. Age can sometimes strain connections, especially when the parties involved no longer have any common events or happenings to share. Therefore, it is necessary to create new shared experiences. This can be anything from picking up a new hobby together to simply watching a weekly television show. The creation of new shared events will replace old memories of times shared. These strategies will permit time spent together with the intent of enjoyment and/or achieving some new goals. Regularly shared experiences are key to the path of continued growth in a relationship. Many strong connections are built on the recollection of the experiences shared together.

The sustained effort of maintaining relationships is ongoing and vital to ensure its strength and durability. Some people put forth little effort into maintaining connections and wonder why over time the relationship seems to wither away. The reality is work and effort is involved in any connection. The lessons that can be learned from putting forth such effort can be seen in the film Annie Hall. Woody Allen's character often told a joke of two elderly women at a resort, one saying "the food here is terrible" and the other responding "yes, and such small portions". Woody's character reflected on this joke to realize that relationships often fail because both parties long stop trying. He concluded that he was often guilty of the same thing with many of his past relationships. "Stopping trying" is a manifestation of laziness in maintaining connections. The relationship has the same old appeal, there is just no drive to manifest its growth.

www.ingramcontent.com/pod-product-compliance
Lightning Source LLC
Chambersburg PA
CBHW031255130726
47988CB00008B/3371